BARRON'S BOOK NOTES

THORNTON WILDER'S

Our Town

BY

W. Meitcke

SERIES COORDINATOR

Murray Bromberg
Principal, Wang High School of Queens
Holliswood, New York

Past President
High School Principals Association of New York City

BARRON'S EDUCATIONAL SERIES, INC.
Woodbury, New York • London • Toronto • Sydney

ACKNOWLEDGMENTS

Our thanks to Milton Katz and Julius Liebb for their advisory assistance on the *Book Notes* series.

Thanks also to Jane O'Sullivan, who made a substantial editorial contribution to this book, and to Charles Steckler, who created three pictures expressly for this book.

All inquiries should be addressed to:
Barron's Educational Series, Inc.
113 Crossways Park Drive
Woodbury, New York 11797

Library of Congress Catalog Card No. 85-3951

International Standard Book No. 0-8120-3533-X

Library of Congress Cataloging in Publication Data

Meitcke, W.
    Thornton Wilder's Our town.

    (Barron's book notes)
    Bibliography: p. 80
    Summary: A guide to reading "Our Town" with a critical and appreciative mind encouraging analysis of plot, style, form, and structure. Also includes background on the author's life and times, sample tests, term paper suggestions, and a reading list.
    1. Wilder, Thornton, 1897–1975. Our town.
[1. Wilder, Thornton, 1897–1975. Our town. 2. American literature—History and criticism] I. Title. II. Series.
PS3545.I345O98   1985   812'.52   85-3951
ISBN 0-7641-9133-0

PRINTED IN THE UNITED STATES OF AMERICA

567   550   987654321

CONTENTS

ADVISORY BOARD

HOW TO USE THIS BOOK

You have to know how to approach literature in order to get the most out of it. This *Barron's Book Notes* volume follows a plan based on methods used by some of the best students to read a work of literature.

Begin with the guide's section on the author's life and times. As you read, try to form a clear picture of the author's personality, circumstances, and motives for writing the work. This background usually will make it easier for you to hear the author's tone of voice, and follow where the author is heading.

Then go over the rest of the introductory material—such sections as those on the plot, characters, setting, themes, and style of the work. Underline, or write down in your notebook, particular things to watch for, such as contrasts between characters and repeated literary devices. At this point, you may want to develop a system of symbols to use in marking your text as you read. (Of course, you should only mark up a book you own, not one that belongs to another person or a school.) Perhaps you will want to use a different letter for each character's name, a different number for each major theme of the book, a different color for each important symbol or literary device. Be prepared to mark up the pages of your book as you read. Put your marks in the margins so you can find them again easily.

Now comes the moment you've been waiting for—the time to start reading the work of literature. You may want to put aside your *Barron's Book Notes* volume until you've read the work all the way through. Or you may want to alternate, reading the *Book Notes* analysis of each section as soon as you have

finished reading the corresponding part of the original. Before you move on, reread crucial passages you don't fully understand. (Don't take this guide's analysis for granted—make up your own mind as to what the work means.)

Once you've finished the whole work of literature, you may want to review it right away, so you can firm up your ideas about what it means. You may want to leaf through the book concentrating on passages you marked in reference to one character or one theme. This is also a good time to reread the *Book Notes* introductory material, which pulls together insights on specific topics.

When it comes time to prepare for a test or to write a paper, you'll already have formed ideas about the work. You'll be able to go back through it, refreshing your memory as to the author's exact words and perspective, so that you can support your opinions with evidence drawn straight from the work. Patterns will emerge, and ideas will fall into place; your essay question or term paper will almost write itself. Give yourself a dry run with one of the sample tests in the guide. These tests present both multiple-choice and essay questions. An accompanying section gives answers to the multiple-choice questions as well as suggestions for writing the essays. If you have to select a term paper topic, you may choose one from the list of suggestions in this book. This guide also provides you with a reading list, to help you when you start research for a term paper, and a selection of provocative comments by critics, to spark your thinking before you write.

THE AUTHOR
AND HIS TIMES

Thornton Wilder was one of the most cosmopolitan and sophisticated of American writers. Born in the Midwest on April 17, 1897, he was educated in China, in German language schools, in America, and in Rome. He was thoroughly familiar with classical literature, translated and adapted the Norwegian playwright Henrik Ibsen, and was an enthusiastic supporter of the noted novelist James Joyce at a time when the general public dismissed the Irish writer as incomprehensible, obscene, or both. In 1938, before *Our Town* opened, Wilder was a critically acclaimed writer and a member in good standing of U.S. intellectual circles. The day it opened, he was the author of a smash hit, a play that has been enormously popular in both the United States and Europe ever since. In fact, it is quite possible that almost any day of the year you can find *Our Town* being performed somewhere by either a professional or an amateur group.

How did this happen? How did the intellectual Wilder produce a play as straightforward and "folksy" as *Our Town*? How did the admirer of the avant-garde and experimental works of Joyce produce this nostalgic look at "the good old days"? Perhaps the play isn't as simple as it might appear at first glance. Before we begin looking at the play, let's take a look at the author.

Wilder was born in Madison, Wisconsin, where his father owned and edited a local newspaper.

The Wilders were a family dedicated to both religion and intellectual pursuits. Amos Wilder, Thornton's strict father, took firm command of the children's upbringing and education. His decisions were not to be questioned, but they were decisions that provided his children, and Thornton in particular, with an education of both breadth and depth.

In 1906, Amos Wilder was appointed the U.S. consul general in Hong Kong, and Thornton's travels began. For the next nine years the young Wilder's schooling alternated between German and mission schools in China and ordinary public schools in California. He graduated from high school having seen more of the world than most people ever see.

When it was time for college, Wilder wanted to go to Yale, his father's alma mater. Amos, however, was afraid that Yale was too worldly, and instead sent his son to Oberlin, trusting to its reputation as a strongly religious school. Oberlin was also a stimulating college, and Wilder developed a lasting enthusiasm for theater, music, and classical literature. Nonetheless, after two years Thornton transferred to Yale—his family was now living in New Haven, where Yale is located. After a brief stint in the Coast Artillery during World War I, he was graduated in 1920.

Next came several months in Rome, where Wilder took courses in archaeology at the American Academy. This period seems to have had an importance to Wilder out of all proportion to its length. During the course of his studies in Rome, he developed a notion of time that became an important theme in many of his works. After helping excavate an

Etruscan street, exposing bits of the daily lives of people who had lived nearly 3000 years previously, he was struck by the notion that limits of time and geography were false. Past, present, and future should not be considered separately. An American shovel digs into a Roman street and exposes an ancient civilization. "It is only in appearance that time is a river," Wilder wrote later. "It is a vast landscape, and it is the eye of the beholder that moves." As you will see, this view of time, with past, present, and future all existing at once, is important in *Our Town*.

Amos Wilder intervened again and called his son back to America. He had found Thornton a job teaching French at the Lawrenceville School, a famous preparatory school near Princeton, New Jersey. Wilder wrote in his spare time, publishing his first novel, *The Cabala*, and seeing a production of his first full-length play, *The Trumpet Shall Sound*, in 1926. He then wrote the novel *The Bridge of San Luis Rey*. It was a popular and a critical success, a best-seller that won a 1928 Pulitzer Prize. The novel deals with a disparate group of five travelers who are linked when they all die in the collapse of a bridge in 18th-century Peru.

Now financially secure, Wilder quit his job to become a full-time writer, but occasionally did some teaching. He spent two years touring Europe, paying special attention to the European theater.

When Wilder returned to the United States in 1930, the unusual mixture of enthusiasm and weariness, of optimism and disillusion that had characterized the outlook of many persons in the 1920s, was over. The stock market had crashed in 1929 and the Great Depression had begun. Writing about social issues was the order of the day among many influential authors, and Wilder's next book, *The Woman of Andros*, was not a success. It was set in pre-Christian Greece and based on a comedy by the second-century-B.C. Roman playwright Terence. Readers felt it was simply an evasion of reality.

During the next decade, Wilder taught comparative literature at the University of Chicago and became increasingly involved with the theater, particularly in its more experimental aspects. He published a volume of short plays and a novel, American in theme and setting. In several of the plays Wilder experimented with the absence of scenery and the time shifts that he later used in *Our Town*.

The 1930s was a decade of hard times for almost everyone. Millions were out of work, and millions more lived in poverty. Men rode freight trains looking for jobs or handouts, hungry people formed long lines outside soup kitchens, bankrupt farmers gathered what belongings they had and fled the Dust Bowl, and families lived on potato soup and considered themselves lucky. At the same time, the arts flourished. The theme of social injustice roused the passions of writers, in novels and in plays. As the decade drew to an end, and the German dictator Adolf Hitler's power grew stronger in Europe, possible involvement in war was added to the frustrations of Americans. To most people, things did not look good.

Then came 1938 and *Our Town*, Wilder's first hit play and the source of his second Pulitzer Prize. Its enormous success was something of a surprise to both Wilder and his collaborators. His friends all thought it was good but didn't expect much of a run for it. During its Boston tryouts, audiences obviously thought it was much too sad, and the producers brought it to New York early for fear it would be washed out in a sea of tears if they left it on the road. Then, instead of the modest critical success everyone expected, the play was a smash hit. Critics raved and audiences loved it. A movie version followed shortly, and *Our Town* became one of the standbys of amateur dramatic groups.

The play wasn't, of course, equally popular with everyone. Although Wilder won a Pulitzer Prize for his play, the New York Drama Critics gave their award to John Steinbeck's *Of Mice and Men*, a play somewhat more concerned with social themes. And part of the popularity of *Our Town* may be due to misunderstandings of Wilder's intentions. When *Our Town* was being turned into a movie, Wilder was constantly being frustrated by changes the producer was making. The producer wanted to add costumes and scenery to make things more realistic, and Wilder objected that this would make the play trite. Little homey touches were added, and Wilder complained that the audience would feel justified in feeling they were watching pictures of "Quaint Hayseed Family Life."

However, there has always been appreciation of Wilder's serious philosophical concerns in *Our Town* and admiration for his use of theatrical techniques. The play has been particularly admired in Europe. The Swiss playwright Friedrich Dürrenmatt, author of *The Visit* (1958), a bitter allegory about the nature of evil, rather surprisingly cites *Our Town* as one of his major influences.

Wilder's influence can also be seen in the Theater of the Absurd movement of the 1960s. In those plays there is little action, hardly any scenery, and the dialog is based on philosophical ideas. Edward Albee, the best-known of the U.S. absurdist playwrights, incorporates all of these theatrical techniques into his work. Albee, who wrote *Who's Afraid of Virginia Woolf* (1962), says that Thornton Wilder advised him to give up struggling over writing poetry and become a playwright. Albee took years to follow Wilder's suggestion, but went on to have a successful career using many of Wilder's theatrical techniques.

Wilder's next play after *Our Town*, called *The Merchant of Yonkers*, was also produced in 1938, but ran for only 39 performances. Wilder later revised it and, as *The Matchmaker*, it was a Broadway success in 1954. *The Matchmaker* was the inspiration for the musical comedy *Hello, Dolly!*, one of the longest running shows in Broadway history and also a successful motion picture.

In 1943, Wilder, now a major in the Army Air Forces, won his third Pulitzer Prize, for *The Skin of Our Teeth*. This unusual play, which tells how the Antrobus family of Excelsior, New Jersey, manages to survive the Ice Age, was both successful and controversial. Several critics accused Wilder of plagiarism, claiming he borrowed large parts of the play from *Finnegan's Wake*, a novel by James Joyce.

Wilder's other works include *The Ides of March* (1948), a historical novel about the last days of Julius Caesar, and *The Eighth Day* (1967), a novel, set in the United States and Latin America, dealing with the effects of an act of violence on a growing number of persons. *The Eighth Day* won a prestigious National Book Award in 1968.

In recognition of his important contributions to American writing, Wilder in 1965 was awarded the first National Medal of Literature. He died on December 7, 1975, at Hamden, Connecticut.

THE PLAY

The Plot

The plot of *Our Town* is rather simple. In fact, some readers say there is no plot, that what passes for a story is simply a few anecdotes illustrating life in Grover's Corners. Straightforward as it is, the story has always had great appeal. After all, where would novels and plays be, where would movies and television be, if you didn't have stories about people falling in love and getting married?

This simple story begins at daybreak. Act I is Daily Life. The Stage Manager tells you that you are in Grover's Corners, New Hampshire, in 1901. He tells you a bit about the town and points out the homes of the two families you will see most of, the Webbs and the Gibbses. Then the people begin to appear. Dr. Gibbs comes home from delivering twins. The mothers call the children to breakfast and get them ready and off to school. Then the two mothers stop for a bit of gossip while they work.

The Stage Manager interrupts with some more information about the town, and then the children come home from school. Emily Webb promises to give George Gibbs some help with his homework. Back to the Stage Manager for some information about other people in the town, and then it's evening, and you can hear the choir practicing at the Congregational church. George and his father have a "serious" talk, and Mrs. Gibbs tells her husband the gossip about the drunken organist, Simon

Stimson. The town constable comes by to check that all is well, and the Stage Manager calls an end to this typical day in Grover's Corners.

The Stage Manager tells you that Act II will be Love and Marriage. It isn't much of a surprise to discover that George and Emily are the ones who will marry. The Stage Manager interrupts, as usual, this time to take you back to a scene from George and Emily's courtship and the Gibbs' reaction to George's plans. Then, after a few more philosophical observations, the Stage Manager takes you to the wedding, and everyone is happy.

Act III opens in the graveyard, and the Stage Manager tells you that nine years have passed. A new grave is being prepared, and you soon discover that Emily is the one who has died. She joins the dead already resting in the graveyard, including her mother-in-law, Mrs. Gibbs, but she is still restless. Despite all the warnings, she chooses to go back, to see her twelfth birthday. But it's too painful. She can't stand watching everyone pay so little attention to life and flees back to her place among the dead. Night comes to Grover's Corners, and the Stage Manager wishes the audience a good night, too.

The Characters

Wilder knew a great deal about the theater, both its literary history and its practical problems. He had a number of friends who were actors or directors, and he knew that part of any play would be created by them. Instead of viewing this as a drawback—actors distorting his work of art—he thought of it as an asset. The actors collaborated with the playwright in creating the finished performance.

A few years after *Our Town,* Wilder wrote:

> Characterization in a play is like a blank check which the dramatist accords to the actor for him to fill in—not entirely blank, for a number of indications of individuality are already there, but to a far less definite and absolute degree than in the novel. . . . The dramatist's principal interest being the movement of the story, he is willing to resign the more detailed aspects of the characterization to the actor.

In *Our Town,* the actors have plenty of room for their own characterizations to fit in, because Wilder has created types rather than individuals. George, Emily, and all the people in Grover's Corners are never very distinctly individual. This means that when you read or see the play, you can keep saying to yourself, "Oh, yes. I know someone like that. He's just like so-and-so." More important, you can say to yourself, "I know what he's feeling. I've felt like that myself."

By keeping characterization at a minimum, Wilder also warns you that what is important here is ideas, not personalities; universals, not individuals.

The Stage Manager
The most important character in the play is the Stage Manager, who has no name and has only a minor role in the flow of the story. Yet he has by far the longest part in the play, the most speeches, and he is always on the stage.

He speaks in a folksy manner, just chatting with the audience, making homey observations and sounding very commonsensical. He may sound unsophisticated, but his ancestry as a character goes way back to the chorus in ancient Greek drama, and he has relatives in medieval and renaissance plays as well.

In ancient Greece, plays first appeared as part of religious festivals. They were very stylized and ritualistic. Important in each play was the chorus, generally a group of neutral observers who commented on the action and told the audience about events that happened offstage. The chorus frequently advised the audience how they were supposed to react to events on stage and reinforced the moral message of the play. Characters serving a similar function can also be found in the religious plays of the Middle Ages.

Indeed, until naturalism began to predominate on the stage in the nineteenth century, characters in plays frequently addressed the audience directly in asides. Everyone assumed that if you were in the audience you knew you were watching a play. Wilder uses the Stage Manager to make this idea clear in *Our Town*. The constant intervention of the Stage Manager, his halting of the action, his moving back and forth in time, make it clear that what you are watching is not "reality" in the naturalistic sense.

One of the major questions you will have to answer for yourself as you read this play is how much importance you should give to the Stage Manager. Is he a genial old codger, a sort of Spirit of Grover's Corners, giving you a somewhat sentimental picture of life in small-town America? Is he the spokesman for the author's views? Is he speaking seriously about "the meaning of life"? Does he represent God? Wilder was a religious writer, though not dogmatic. In the play, the Stage Manager has the power to move time backward and forward, and he knows what is yet to be. Although he is always there, the living characters never seem to be aware of his existence.

Emily Webb
Emily is the daughter of the editor of the town newspaper. She marries George Gibbs and dies giving birth to their second child. She is the girl who grows up during the course of the play, both in age and understanding. In Act III she has the famous life-affirming speech, "Oh, earth, you're too wonderful for anybody to realize you." At the end, speaking of the living, she says, "They don't understand much, do they?"

Emily's speeches at the end of the play are so obviously important that they suggest that you should have been paying special attention to her all through the play. And it's hard not to pay attention to her. From her first appearance she's so full of enthusiasm audiences find it impossible not to like her. And the very familiarity of her emotions make them all the more real. Was there ever an adolescent who could look at the moonlight unmoved? Is there anything strange about a girl who's jealous of a boy's love for sports? Did any bride ever approach her wedding without a last minute moment of panic?

When you first see Emily, she's a schoolgirl having breakfast and engaging in a bit of one-upmanship with her younger brother. She's proud of the fact that she does well in school and daydreams about being a great lady. But she can't keep it up too long with George, and her conversation with her mother shows that what she would really like is to be beautiful. Come evening, she tries to help George with his homework—it obviously isn't very helpful help—but what she really wants to do is dream in the moonlight. In short, she's a young girl growing up.

In Act II you see that she is a bit miffed with George, who has been ignoring her for baseball. But once she gets a hint that he loves her, she is perfectly willing to overlook his failings and rank him with such "perfect" men as her father and his. When it comes time for her wedding, she has a moment of panic, when being Daddy's Little Girl seems so much safer than being a grownup wife and mother. But the moment passes, and she does grow up.

In Act III, Emily undergoes the third step in her metamorphosis, moving from life to death. But is the change a loss or a gain? She always seemed particularly aware of the world around her, yet when she returns to her twelfth birthday, she is overwhelmed by all that she and those she loves ignored all the time.

George Gibbs

George, the son of Dr. Gibbs, is the boy next door who marries Emily. If she is a typical American girl, he is a typical American boy—or at least what many people think of as typical. He is nice and polite, though not too bright; loving, but not very good at expressing his emotions; and perfectly happy to stay down on the farm.

He goes through the same stages of growing up that Emily does, but he's always lagging a bit behind her in maturity as well as in math. While

Emily is acting out the great lady, he's tossing a baseball, too shy to talk to her except by "accident." He wants to be a farmer when he grows up and can't imagine having any trouble doing the work on a farm, though he still has a bit of trouble getting around to chopping wood for his mother at home. And he isn't hypnotized by the moonlight until Emily points it out to him.

When it comes to courting Emily, he's more than a little tongue-tied (not an unusual state of mind for a young person in love). But Emily, who has no trouble telling George what's wrong with him, also has no trouble understanding what he means, even if he can't manage to actually say that he loves her.

In Act III George doesn't say a word, but he has his most powerful scene when he throws himself on Emily's grave. Once more, Emily has gone before him—she has died, and she also understands more than he does.

George and Emily aren't rebels; they don't want to change the world. They get along well with their parents and aren't troubled by a generation gap. They're "normal" and "typical" and "nice"—perhaps you'll find them a bit idealized. The boy and girl next door fall in love, marry, and live happily until death parts them. It's an old story, and it's been told many times because it happens to so many people. If you can understand how George and Emily feel, if you can identify with them, then Wilder has at least partially succeeded in what he was trying to do.

Dr. Frank Gibbs

The kindly country physician, Doc Gibbs is also the loving husband and kindly father who can scold his son and raise his allowance at the same time. He seems to know about and like everyone in town. He has sympathy for the town drunk, and won't either condemn him or interfere. Doc Gibbs is perfectly happy at home in Grover's Corners and has no desire to travel any farther than Gettysburg, Pennsylvania, where he can reexamine the famous Civil War battlefield.

Mr. Charles Webb

Mr. Webb is the editor of the local newspaper, and his hobby is studying Napoleon, not the Civil War. Otherwise, he's very much like Doc Gibbs. You see them both as fathers and husbands, and as kindly and tolerant citizens of Grover's Corners. Both of them manage to keep their sense of humor, even under the strain of their children's wedding. You may feel the speeches of one could easily be spoken by the other.

Julia Hersey Gibbs

Mrs. Gibbs is Doc Gibbs's wife and the mother of George and Rebecca. And that's what she is, a wife and mother. She worries about her husband's health, she worries about her children's health, and wonders how her son George will ever remember to put on warm clothes once he's married. She spends her life taking care of others. Although she has a dream of visiting Paris, with some money she could get by selling a family heirloom, she leaves the money to George and Emily, who use it to build a new barn and buy a cement drinking fountain for the animals. Even at the end, she is in a sense taking care of Emily, giving her advice about her new existence.

Myrtle Webb

Like her neighbor Mrs. Gibbs, Mrs. Webb is a wife and mother, taking care of a husband and children. Her distinction is that she was once the second prettiest girl in town. But that is not really any more important to her than going to Paris is to Mrs. Gibbs. Many readers find the two women, like their husbands, virtually interchangeable. You probably can't tell them apart by their speeches. What kind of comment does Wilder seem to be making about women with these two characters? Is it different from the kind of comment he is making about men with Doc Gibbs and Mr. Webb?

Rebecca Gibbs and Wally Webb

Rebecca is George's younger sister, and Wally is Emily's younger brother. You never know very much about them as personalities. You only see them as children having typical squabbles with their siblings. Wally dies young, on a boy scout trip, and Rebecca marries and moves to Ohio.

Simon Stimson

The church organist who drinks too much, Stimson has the distinction of being the only person you meet in Grover's Corners who is unhappy. Doc Gibbs refers to the sorrow in Stimson's life, but never tells you what it is. Stimson doesn't fit in, but you never know why. Ultimately, he hangs himself, and in the graveyard at the end, his words are the only bitter comments about life.

Louella Soames

Mrs. Soames, the town gossip, has plenty to say about Simon Stimson's misconduct (all of it bad).

But she's also an enthusiastic wedding guest, and among the dead she is still a chatterbox. In contrast to Stimson, she remembers that life was wonderful as well as awful.

Joe Crowell and Si Crowell
Joe and later his brother Si are the town's newspaper boys, appearing early in the morning. Neither is very enthusiastic about marriage, which deprives the world first of a schoolteacher and later of the town's best baseball player. You are told that Joe is very bright, but dies in France during World War I. You never see much of either boy, however.

Howie Newsome
Howie and his horse Bessie deliver the milk and the gossip every morning. In small towns, the milkman was a traditional carrier of local news, since he stopped frequently at almost every house. Howie is friendly and chatty.

Joe Stoddard and Sam Craig
In the last act of *Our Town*, Joe Stoddard and Sam Craig replace the newsboy and the milkman. Instead of bringing news of life, they bring news of death. Joe is the undertaker, and Sam is a local boy who had moved away. Between them, they fill you in on recent deaths and their effect on people in the town. They have little individuality.

Constable Warren
You never hear of any crime in Grover's Corners to keep Constable Warren busy. Instead, he watches over the safety of the townspeople, making sure boys like Wally don't start smoking, and making

sure Stimson gets home safe and sound without noticing that anyone is watching him. You'll probably see Constable Warren as a benign spirit taking care of the town.

Other Elements
SETTING

You could say that *Our Town* has two settings. One is the town of Grover's Corners. The other is the stage on which the play is being performed. You can't ignore either one.

Grover's Corners has a very specific location. It's not just in New Hampshire, for the Stage Manager also gives you its latitude and longitude. For an imaginary town it has a very exact place on the globe. It has a history as well. Not a history of great men—the Stage Manager says the town never had them—but a geological and anthropological history, taking you hundreds of millions of years into the past.

The Stage Manager also gives you a date for the first act—May 7, 1901. This is the good old days. It was even the good old days in 1938 when *Our Town* was first performed—the days before the national economy dominated most every part of the country, before World War I transformed the world. But again it is a very specific date, just as it is a very specific location.

At the same time you should note that the play is called *Our Town*, not *A Town*. This is where the bare stage comes in. Wilder uses it to make clear that he is really talking about everyone's town, just as he is talking about universal feelings and emotions, about human life in general, rather than about a few specific lives.

Wilder knew that every person who lives encounters birth, love, and death. You know it, too. By stripping the stage of the trappings of naturalism, the realistic scenery and costumes generally found on the stage then (and now), Wilder emphasizes the symbolic nature of the play, its location, and its characters.

"When you emphasize place in the theater," Wilder said, "you drag down and limit and harness time to it." By not having the stage represent any one specific era, the play transcends any particular time and represents all times.

Wilder had some definite notions about the nature of time. One of the major differences between a novel and a play, he pointed out, was that a novel takes place in the past, but a play always takes place in the present. Although it may be 1901 in Grover's Corners, it is also today on the stage whenever the play is being performed.

THEMES

The following are major themes of *Our Town*.

1. THE IMPORTANCE OF LOVE

Love is mentioned often in *Our Town*, and it is illustrated many times. The major characters all love one another, and as the play progresses you are given examples of different types of love.

In Act I you see family love and friendship. Parents and children love each other and neighbors love each other, just as ideally they should. In Act II, you see romantic love, culminating in marriage, again as ideally it should. In Act III you see the kind of love that is perhaps hardest to understand, spiritual, selfless love, love that expects no return.

2.   THE CONTINUITY OF HUMAN LIFE

Over and over in the play you are reminded of the repetition of the cycle of life. The play begins with the birth of twins in Polish town and ends with Emily's death in childbirth. Yet she leaves another child behind, a part of her, just as she goes to join her predecessors in the graveyard on the hill.

Notice the Stage Manager's comments throughout the play. He continually refers to things that happen over and over, to the ways people behave, generation after generation. Look at his comments about the wedding in particular. Can you see why he mentions both the ancestors and the future generations?

3.   THE BEAUTY OF LIFE

You'll probably find Wilder's enthusiasm for life the most obvious theme in *Our Town*. He said that the play is "an attempt to find a value above all price for the smallest events in our daily life." This theme seems the most important reason for the play's popularity. At the same time, it is responsible for most of the criticism that attacks the play as being overly sentimental.

Is the play a valid celebration of the beauty of life? Does Wilder successfully point out the marvels of everyday existence that are ignored by most people and realized only sometimes by poets and saints? Or is the play a sentimental cop-out? Has Wilder made it easy to talk about the wonders of life by omitting the problem of evil from his play? Keep these questions in mind as you read the play.

4. THE MEANING OF LIFE

Wilder is often considered a religious writer, and *Our Town* is considered by many to be a religious play. Can you see why? Consider how often churches are mentioned, how often you hear religious hymns being sung. Is this just one of the realistic details put into the play? Probably not. After all, there was probably a general store in a town like this, too, but Wilder doesn't mention one.

We mentioned the interpretation of the Stage Manager as God in The Characters section. You might also look at his speech at the beginning of Act III. "Everybody knows that *something* is eternal," he says. Wilder may not say what the meaning of life is, but he certainly seems to suggest that there is a meaning.

5. THE UNIVERSAL VS. THE PARTICULAR

Here you have to deal with a question about the nature of reality. In *Our Town*, Wilder seems to be forcing the reader or the audience to see the characters as representing human nature in general. Do you remember Rebecca's speech about her friend's letter, with the address giving her a place in the universe? Did you notice how often the words "hundreds" and "thousands" and "millions" are used in the play? These details suggest that the characters should be understood as part of a greater reality, as part of human existence, not just as part of Grover's Corners. Can you think of any other devices Wilder uses to give a larger context to the play?

6. THE NATURE OF TIME

Wilder thought of past, present, and future all

existing at the same time, though people can only see one moment of it at a particular instant. In *Our Town*, however, he shows different times existing together. For example, when you walk into the theater, the man who turns out to be the Stage Manager is standing there in the present, but he tells you that it is 1901. Later, he interrupts the wedding preparations to send the characters back to their courtship. You'll want to reflect on the importance of this idea in the play.

STYLE

Style involves the way a writer uses language. Wilder was extremely conscious of the sounds and beauty of words as he put them on paper. In fact, his earliest attempts at writing have been criticized because they were "beautiful" but had no substance. As he matured, he outgrew his fondness for "fine writing" and developed an ear for the "right" word. The right word is not necessarily the beautiful one or the fancy one. It's the word that expresses exactly what you want to say. For a playwright, it's the word that is exactly the one a particular character would use in a particular situation.

Wilder was a very conscientious writer. This may be one of the reasons he wrote relatively little. In *Our Town* he accomplishes something of a tour de force. The entire play is written in a dialect that was not Wilder's normal speech. In his letters and essays he used far more formal language.

Why, then, did he write the play in this colloquial, folksy style? Part of the reason is obviously that this would be the normal speech of the residents of Grover's Corners. But why make it the normal speech of the Stage Manager as well? There are a number of possible reasons.

1.   Wilder wanted to make clear that we are all ordinary people by having all his characters speak in ordinary language.

2.   Wilder wanted to make it clear that the Stage Manager did not represent the author by having the Stage Manager speak the language of Grover's Corners, not the language of a Yale graduate.

3.   Because the play is a celebration of everyday life, everyday speech is most appropriate.

Do any of these explanations appeal to you? Can you think of others?

When the play was being prepared for its New York opening in 1938, Wilder had frequent struggles with its producer, Jed Harris. Wilder kept trying to defend his "beautiful prose," while Harris argued that "prose doesn't play." Writing to a friend shortly before the opening, Wilder said, "As long as his [Harris's] suggestions for alterations are on the structure they are often very good; but once they apply to the words, they are always bad and sometimes atrocious."

Judging from the final result, Wilder must have won the battle over words. The language of the play is simple, natural, and frequently very beautiful. What could be more effective than the simple and homey images of Emily's speech as she bids farewell to the world?

POINT OF VIEW

The story in a novel is usually told either by a character, who acts as narrator, or by the all-know-ing author, the omniscient or partially omniscient narrator. For example, in Mark Twain's *Huckleberry Finn,* Huck tells his own story, but in Charles Dickens's *Tale of Two Cities,* it is the omniscient narrator who tells you, "It was the best of times, it was the worst of times. . . ." The narrator is important because you only know what the narrator tells you, and the outlook of the narrator usually affects the way you interpret the story.

In most plays there is no narrator. The evidence is placed directly in front of you, with no interpreter telling you what it all means. *Our Town* is unusual. The play is narrated by the Stage Manager.

Wilder uses this character to give information about the town and its residents the way he would use a narrator in a novel. The Stage Manager knows the past, present, and future. He knows what the characters are feeling, and he tells you what to notice and why. He tells you what he believes is the truth.

But you have the same problem here that you have in a novel. How much of what the Stage Manager says are you going to accept? You can obviously accept what he says about the town and its residents. But do you also accept the philosophy he offers? Do you believe that love is as important as he says? Do you think it's true that people miss the beauty of life? Do you agree that all people are connected in time?

Do you think Wilder intends you to accept what the Stage Manager says? Or is the Stage Manager just another character with his own limitations?

FORM AND STRUCTURE

In contrast to the very conventional and traditional characters and story in *Our Town,* the structure of the play frequently violates modern tradition and convention. As soon as you walk into the theater, you know this will not be the kind of play you're accustomed to seeing. The curtain is up, and you're looking at a bare stage, no scenery at all, just someone who looks like a stagehand dragging some tables and chairs around. You couldn't be blamed for thinking that you've come on the wrong night—that the play is still in rehearsal.

Once the play begins, the Stage Manager often reminds you that it *is* a play. Even his title emphasizes this. You are never allowed to think—at least for very long—that you are watching a slice-of-life, unique events that could only happen once. You are forced to recognize that these characters and events represent what the author sees as universal, not particular, truths. The form of the play has a definite purpose.

Some readers have also noticed the influence of Wilder's classical training. The similarity of the Stage Manager to the ancient Greek chorus has been discussed in The Characters section of this guide. Partly because the Stage Manager performs some of the functions of a Greek chorus, Wilder does not divide acts into the scenes that are typical of modern plays. In addition, the play seems to follow the three unities of Greek drama: unity of time, place, and action.

Unity of time usually means that the entire action of the play takes place within twenty-four hours. In one sense, quite a bit of time is covered in *Our Town*, including shifts backward and forward. In another sense, it all takes place in one day: Act I begins at daybreak and Act III ends at night, a single day of life.

As for unity of place, the location of the play

doesn't change. It is all Grover's Corners (or, if you like, it is all the stage of the theater). And the action is unified in that no subplots complicate the story. (Some people say there isn't a real story at all. Do you agree with them?)

The Story

In order to feel the power of *Our Town*, you should try to imagine the play being presented in front of you. Plays are intended to be performed, and a playwright's intentions are often clearer on stage than on the printed page. This is particularly true in the case of Thornton Wilder's plays, because he considered the actors as collaborators in producing the final product.

ACT I

Our Town begins while people are still entering the theater and being seated. A character known only as the Stage Manager enters a bare, partly lit stage. He puts a table and three chairs stage left and another table and chairs stage right. Then he adds a low bench stage left.

NOTE: *Pullman Car Hiawatha*   Wilder's one-act play, *Pullman Car Hiawatha*, published in 1931, contains many similarities to *Our Town*. Like *Our Town*, the earlier play uses a Stage Manager to set the scene and chat with the audience about the action on stage. The title of *Pullman Car Hiawatha*, refers to a railroad sleeping car named after the legend-

"This play is called *Our Town*."

Charles Steckler

ary Onondaga Indian chief, Hiawatha. The train is
on the New York to Chicago run and Wilder uses
the train, its passengers, and the towns it passes
through to represent the whole of the human experience, in much the same way he uses Grover's
Corners in *Our Town*. In fact, one of the towns
along the route is Grover's Corners, Ohio!

There is little scenery in *Pullman Car Hiawatha;*
the Stage Manager draws outlines of the car and
its compartments on the stage floor with chalk and
passengers enter carrying their own chairs. The
themes of time, size—from the tiniest town to the
entire solar system—death, and repeating cycles
of human activity are all found in this short play.
You might want to read *Pullman Car Hiawatha* and
compare Wilder's treatment of these themes to how
he deals with them in *Our Town*.

After he finishes setting up, the Stage Manager
leans against the wall at the side of the stage and
watches the audience.

NOTE: In a famous speech in William Shakespeare's *As You Like It*, one of the characters says,
"All the world's a stage,/And all the men and
women merely players." Is the Stage Manager indicating to you that the same metaphor is being
used here?

The house lights dim and the Stage Manager
begins to speak. At this point, if you were in the
audience and didn't know anything about the play,

you might be a little confused. You probably would think that the man was just someone working in the theater, not part of the play. Then the first thing he tells you is what you probably just read in your program—who wrote the play, who directed it, who's playing what part. You aren't being allowed to forget that this is a play, not real life.

Then the Stage Manager takes you to Grover's Corners, New Hampshire, just before dawn on May 7, 1901. He describes the town, pointing to different parts of the stage. "Up here is Main Street. . . . Here's the Town Hall and Post Office combined. . . . "

NOTE: Keep in mind that the Stage Manager is talking about a bare stage. You must picture the town for yourself. Wilder didn't want you to sit back passively to watch his play. He wanted you to fill in the setting by using your own imagination and experience. This is unusual in a twentieth-century play. But plays in ancient Greece were staged without scenery, and there were virtually no stage props around 1600, when Shakespeare wrote his great plays.

As he's describing the town, the Stage Manager says something odd: "First automobile's going to come along in about five years, belonged to Banker Cartwright, our richest citizen . . . lives in the big white house up on the hill." Notice the way the verb tenses keep shifting. This is your first hint that something strange is happening with time in this play.

The Stage Manager continues to describe the town, pointing out Doc Gibbs's house, then Editor Webb's house, then the cemetery. This juxtaposition of life and death is obviously important in the play. It's repeated almost immediately: the Stage Manager points out Doc Gibbs, coming on the stage. First he tells you that Doc Gibbs is just coming home from delivering twins, and then he tells you that Doc Gibbs died in 1930. He adds that Mrs. Gibbs died first, "long time ago, in fact." But you can see Mrs. Gibbs on stage. What time is it supposed to be, anyway? Is it 1901, or is it today? Or is it both?

While the Stage Manager points out Doc Gibbs's house, the stagehands push a pair of trellises onto the stage. "For those who think they have to have scenery," the Stage Manager comments. It's a joke, but it's also a reminder of Wilder's theories about the theater.

You also hear a train whistle; the Stage Manager checks his watch and nods to the audience.

NOTE: On sound   Throughout *Our Town* there are stage directions for various sounds. One reason is that Wilder wants to encourage you to use your imagination while watching this play, and sound is a great trigger for imagination. Most people have heard a train whistle—though perhaps not as many now as in 1938—and hearing that sound calls up a response from your unique personal history. By forcing you to remember through the use of one of your senses, Wilder makes your involvement in the play that much greater.

Notice, however, that Wilder does not include

stage directions for all the possible sounds in Grover's Corners. You might want to make one list of the sound effects called for in the script and another of the sound effects that could have been included but weren't. What conclusions can you draw from comparing the lists?

Before anything happens, before any of the characters actually say or do anything, the Stage Manager has talked for a long time. Why do you suppose this is so? He has set the stage for you and established a gentle, friendly tone for the play. But in most plays that is accomplished with the scenery. You can tell where you are and what kind of play this is going to be as soon as the curtain rises. What else is Wilder doing with the Stage Manager?

Finally, something happens. The earlybirds of the town appear—the newsboy and the milkman are starting their rounds and the doctor is finishing his. They stop for a brief exchange of gossip—the schoolteacher is getting married, the doctor just delivered twins, and the milkman's horse can't adapt to a change in route.

While this is going on, Mrs. Webb and Mrs. Gibbs are in their kitchens, pantomiming the preparations for breakfast. Remember that if you were seeing the play you'd be watching the pantomimes and listening to the conversation at the same time. Perhaps Wilder is pointing out that life doesn't happen in just one place at just one time.

NOTE: Pantomime can be a particularly effective stage technique. It draws an audience into the action and encourages observers to use their imaginations more actively. Try it for yourself. Take turns with friends miming some common activity. How do you feel as you watch? Do you pay more attention than you usually would? Do you notice things you would normally ignore?

Now it's breakfast time, and the children must prepare for school. Mrs. Gibbs is calling George and Rebecca; Mrs. Webb is calling Emily and Wally. The conversation may not sparkle but it probably sounds familiar to you. Mrs. Gibbs complains to her husband that George isn't helping with the chores. Mrs. Webb reminds Wally to wash thoroughly. Rebecca doesn't want to wear her blue gingham dress—that's the one she hates. George wants a raise in his allowance. Children are reminded to eat slowly, finish their breakfast, stand up straight, pick up their feet.

Does it sound familiar? Although the scene takes place at the start of the twentieth century, the conversation is almost timeless. Once upon a time there was probably a Neanderthal girl complaining that she didn't like her wolfskin robe and a Neanderthal mother telling her children to gnaw their bones slowly. And if you listen tomorrow morning, you may hear a similar conversation in your own house. Did anyone ever tell you to come when called? Did anyone ever remind you to do your chores? To stand up straight? To finish your breakfast?

The next question, of course, is why did Wilder use such ordinary conversation for this scene? Does it help you identify with the characters? Even if it doesn't sound familiar, does it sound appealing?

Would you like to grow up in a town like this, in
a family like one of these?

Breakfast over, Mrs. Webb fills her apron and
goes out to feed the chickens. Mrs. Webb goes out
to sit in the garden while she strings her beans.
Mrs. Gibbs comes over to share the task and to
share her secret.

A secondhand furniture man from Boston has
offered Mrs. Gibbs $350 for her old highboy (a chest
of drawers on legs). This is an amazing windfall.
Mrs. Webb thinks it's a wonderful chance, but Mrs.
Gibbs isn't entirely sure she wants the money. The
only thing she really wants is for her husband to
accompany her on a trip to Paris. The problem is
that she doesn't think he'll go. She's dropped a
few hints about "if I got a legacy," but hasn't got-
ten anywhere. Dr. Gibbs says "it might make him
discontented with Grover's Corners to be traipsin'
about Europe." His idea of a perfect vacation is
visiting Civil War battlefields.

Unfortunately for her, Mrs. Gibbs seems a bit
tired of battlefields like Gettysburg and Antietam.
Mrs. Webb urges her to sell the highboy and keep
dropping hints. "That's how I got to see the Atlantic Ocean, y'know."

NOTE: On hints and woman's place Mrs. Webb
suggests that Mrs. Gibbs hint about what she wants
her husband to know, and later you will see her
do just that. Emily will also offer George hints.
Other characters will also speak indirectly. Hinting
is offering an idea in a gentle way, not forcing it
upon a person. Why not come right out and say
what's on your mind? Isn't Mrs. Gibbs missing an

opportunity? In Act III, Emily sees the many ways
we miss the chance to show our love for one another. Is hinting another way we miss the chance
to say "I love you"? Or is it a way we avoid hurting
people's feelings unnecessarily?

This scene also raises some questions about the
role of women in Grover's Corners. At the turn of
the century, women still couldn't vote and most
didn't work outside the home. With the hindsight
gained from the current feminist movement, you
might see Mrs. Gibbs and Mrs. Webb as having
little power or freedom to make their own decisions. How do you think Wilder felt about this? Is
the playwright unconsciously reflecting the major-
ity view of that time? Is he supporting it with an
idealized picture of the mother as the loving and
supportive center of the family? Or is he subtly
criticizing the position in which society placed
women? What evidence can you find in the play
to support your view?

The Stage Manager enters, interrupting the conversation between the two women and sending
them away. This is another reminder that this is a
stage play, not real life.

Wilder constructs reality on the stage in such a
way that the audience can easily relate to what is
taking place. At the same time, he constantly reminds you that this is a theatrical production, a
game that a group of people are playing on the
stage. He wants you to realize that the only things
that are real and important in life happen inside
of you. It's not what's being acted out on the stage
that's important, but how you respond to it. This
idea is crucial in the final act, so keep it in mind.

Now the Stage Manager invites Professor Willard from the State University to sketch in the town's history. Very briefly you go from Archaeozoic granite ("some of the oldest land in the world") to the twins who had just been born when the play began. In between you have the same sort of zigzag, from sandstone outcroppings three hundred million years old to Silas Peckham's cow pasture, from tenth-century Cotahatchee tribes to possible traces in three families.

NOTE: This broad view of the world juxtaposed with a close-up view of the town will be repeated throughout the play. Wilder is commenting on the greatness of the universe, the smallness of daily human existence, and the simultaneous importance of both. Wilder did not see human existence as small or petty in contrast to the vastness of history. Instead, he believed that the humdrum activities of daily life were common to all people in all times, and that this bound humanity into one great living force. The Stage Manager acts as the link between the two concepts. He keeps putting the "action" of the play into proper perspective.

The play begins by showing you the lives of a few people in a small town. By the end, the characters will have become representative of all humanity. Wilder starts with one small idea and expands it until he is dealing with very large ideas. If you are aware of this as you read, you can appreciate how Wilder is able to accomplish it.

The Stage Manager dismisses Willard and asks Editor Webb to come out. Mrs. Webb comes out instead to explain that her husband has just cut his hand and will be right out. Her impatient call, "Charles! Everybody's waitin'," is so believable and typical that you are immediately back in Grover's Corners.

Mr. Webb enters and offers you some statistical information—the kind you'd find in an almanac or a sociology book. He says it's a "very ordinary town." Does it sound ordinary to you? Is the kind of population it has anything like the population in a town you know of?

The Stage Manager calls for questions from the audience (only actors are expected to respond). The Lady in the Balcony asks about drinking. The Belligerent Man asks about social injustice. The Lady in the Box asks about culture. These are all Major Issues, Important Questions, but they aren't of much importance in Grover's Corners. Drinking? There's some, but not enough to make anyone think it's a serious problem. Injustice? Everyone knows it exists, but until someone can figure out a way to eliminate it, the citizens of Grover's Corners are content to help those who need help and otherwise mind their own business. Culture? Love of Beauty? Well, they know their Bible, and in place of art they have the beauty of nature. Why bring this up? What is Wilder's point here? Is he saying that we should all be simple folk and not try to think about culture or social problems? Is he saying that these problems are transitory, that they will be solved, and we should concentrate on eternal, timeless questions? What do you think?

NOTE: Social issues One of the strongest criticisms leveled against Wilder, especially in his early work, was that he was unconcerned about the social and political issues of his day. Some readers believe that he should address current problems like war and poverty. Others say he was concerned not with the particular, but with universal issues of human existence. This is part of an ongoing argument among students of literature. Does the artist have a responsibility to deal with the problems of his society? Or are timeless issues more important? What do you think?

Wilder may have been giving his critics an answer in this scene. In 1901, the "Evils of Drink" was a popular issue, and many social activists sought to completely ban consumption of alcohol. In 1919 the manufacture and sale of alcoholic beverages in the United States was prohibited. In 1933, however, prohibition was ended on the national level after proving less than successful.

The Stage Manager dismisses Mr. Webb and announces a shift in time. Now it is early afternoon. People have had dinner, all the dishes are washed, Mr. Webb is mowing the lawn (in pantomime, remember), and the children are coming home from school. Emily is calling to her friends and walking along pretending that she's a great lady. George is tossing a ball in the air—until he bumps into Mrs. Forrest.

NOTE: The Stage Manager   You have by now seen quite a bit of evidence indicating the unusual nature of the Stage Manager's role. Like the Greek chorus he comments on the action and fills you in on the background, but he has greater power than that. He can call forth and dismiss the characters, control their actions without their even noticing him, stand by invisibly as they go about their daily life, or suddenly become a character like Mrs. Forrest. He interrupts time and moves it up. He could be a frightening character if he were presented in a different tone. Maybe that is partly why Wilder gives him the friendly, folksy speech of Grover's Corners.

On the way home from school, George and Emily stop to talk. Emily is good at school work. George has been watching her doing homework in the evening. She promises to give him some "hints" to help him do his. In return, he confides his ambition to become a farmer.

Emily helps her mother with the string beans and asks one of the questions that often bother young girls: "Am I pretty?" She can't pry a satisfying answer from her mother—no guarantees here of future romance. All Mrs. Webb says is that Emily is "Pretty enough for all normal purposes."

NOTE: Exotic ambitions don't seem to take people very far in Grover's Corners. Mrs. Gibbs never visits Paris—in fact, when she does go away, to see her daughter in Ohio, she dies. Emily doesn't become a fine lady and doesn't spend her life "making speeches." The emphasis here is all on "normal purposes." Why do you suppose this is so?

Now you are back with the Stage Manager again. He tells you about the cornerstone of the new bank. It will have a time capsule in it, so when people a thousand years from now dig it up they will know about Grover's Corners. In it will be a copy of *The New York Times* and of Mr. Webb's *Sentinel*, a Bible, the Constitution of the United States, and a copy of Shakespeare's plays.

Then the Stage Manager says to the audience, "What do you say, folks? What do you think?" He almost sounds like a teacher. But what *do* you think? Would those items tell people a thousand years from now what life was like in Grover's Corners? You might notice that those items cover religion, politics, and culture, the same topics covered by the questions from the audience.

Next comes an important passage, worth reading closely:

> Y'know—Babylon once had two million people in it, and all we know about 'em is the names of the kings and some copies of wheat contracts . . . and contracts for the sale of slaves. Yet every night all those families sat down to supper, and the father came home from his work, and the smoke went up the chimney,—same as here. And even in Greece and Rome, all we know about the *real* life of the people is what we can piece together out of the joking poems and the comedies they wrote for the theatre back then.

Here past, present, and future are being tied together—the people in ancient Babylon, those in Grover's Corners, and the ones a thousand years from now who will look into the time capsule. All are the same when it comes to *real* life. What does Wilder mean by real life? Obviously not the things that find their way into history books, not the Treaty

of Versailles or Lindbergh's solo flight across the
Atlantic. For Wilder, this play, with children doing
homework and mothers stringing beans, is about
the real essence of life.

In that speech the Stage Manager also comments
that what we learn about real life in Greece and
Rome we learn from comedies and joking poems.
Maybe that gives you a hint about the reason for
the tone of this play. The play may deal with enormous themes of life and death, but the tone is most
often friendly, joking.

The choir now begins to sing "Blessed Be the
Tie that Binds." They are being led by Simon Stimson, the choirmaster and organist. Two ladders have
been pushed onto the stage; they suggest the second stories of the two houses. George and Emily
each climb one and pantomime doing homework.
The Stage Manager, still standing at the front of
the stage, tells the audience, "The day's running
down like a tired clock."

NOTE: "Blessed Be the Tie that Binds"   This traditional hymn is used in each of the three acts.
Wilder chose it for its words:

> Blest be the tie that binds
> Our hearts in Christian love:
> The fellowship of kindred minds
> Is like to that above.
>
> Before our Father's throne
> We pour our ardent prayers;
> Our fears, our hopes, our aims are one,
> Our comforts and our cares.

Can you see how this hymn fits in with the themes
of *Our Town*?

Charles Steckler

"I don't see it. Emily, can you give me a hint?"

Against the background of the choir rehearsal, Emily admires the moonlight and George seeks help with his homework. He seems to be having quite a bit of trouble with it. Then Doc Gibbs calls George down for a talk.

George receives a lecture on responsibility. It's a lecture you have probably heard at some time in your life. It may not have been, "How are you going to be able to do all the work on the farm if you can't even remember to chop the wood for your mother?" But how about, "How can you be hungry for dessert when you are too full to finish your vegetables?" Or, "How can you remember the entire TV schedule, but you can't remember what you have for homework?"

It's a very kindly lecture, with far more love than harshness. Part of Doc Gibbs's point is that you do things for people because you love them, not because you will be punished if you don't.

NOTE: The generation gap doesn't seem to exist in Grover's Corners. This isn't because parent-child conflicts hadn't yet been invented. It's because Wilder wants to give you an idealized picture of family life.

Choir practice is over and the ladies come home. Mrs. Webb and Mrs. Gibbs stop to gossip with Mrs. Soames, who seems to enjoy being shocked at Simon Stimson's behavior. He was drunk at choir practice, and it wasn't the first time. Mrs. Webb and Mrs. Gibbs are more charitable, Mrs. Webb saying that he's getting better, not worse.

They finally say good-bye. Mrs. Gibbs returns home, and takes her husband into the garden to enjoy the moonlight—the same moonlight Emily had been admiring earlier. She passes on the gossip about Simon Stimson. It's a situation Doc Gibbs seems to be familiar with, and he suggests that Stimson "ain't made for small-town life. I don't know how that'll end. . . ."

This is the first time the expression "how things will end" is used. You will hear it again. It is one of the play's most haunting refrains. What do you think Wilder's purpose is in repeating the idea?

Why do you suppose Wilder has Doc Gibbs say that Stimson isn't made for small-town life? If Grover's Corners represents the whole world, what other kind of life is there? Is Wilder suggesting that some people aren't able to handle life at all?

Mrs. Gibbs makes some hints about her legacy and hopes for a vacation—though she talks about duty, not desire. But the doctor dismisses the idea and hurries her into the house.

There seems to be things left unsaid here, just as between Emily and her mother. It's not that these people don't love each other, but they seem to have trouble expressing their feelings. You will see more of this later.

The grownups withdraw, and Rebecca climbs the ladder to join her brother—to his irritation. But she wants to enjoy the moonlight too, the same moonlight that Emily and the Gibbses enjoyed, that is shining "on South America, Canada and half the whole world." The same moonlight that Constable Warren and Mr. Webb admire when they meet a moment later as Mr. Webb is on his way home from the newspaper.

The constable and Mr. Webb also encounter Stimson, who appears and departs, silent and unsteady. The constable and Mr. Webb are sympathetic. "He's seen a peck of trouble," says Mr. Webb, but we never know what it was. Then the conversation shifts, and Mr. Webb asks the constable to keep an eye out for Wally, to make sure he doesn't smoke cigarettes.

Again there is a sense of half-completed conversations and missed moments.

Rebecca tells her brother about a letter her friend Jane Crofut got from a minister. The address said: Jane Crofut; The Crofut Farm; Grover's Corners; Sutton County; New Hampshire; United States of America.

George is not impressed. But that's not all, says Rebecca. It goes on: The United States of America, Continent of North America, Western Hemisphere; the Earth; the Solar System; the Universe; the Mind of God.

"What do you know!" exclaims George.

Wilder has taken you again from the trivial to the profound, from children doing homework to the Mind of God. Wilder is reminding you that both the smallest and the greatest exist side by side, and both have to be recognized.

But to end the act on a less solemn note, the Stage Manager steps out to say, "You can go and smoke now, those that smoke."

ACT II

The stage for the second act still has the tables and chairs for the two kitchens, though the ladders and small bench are gone. Again the Stage Manager has been watching the audience settle down.

"Three years have gone by. Yes, the sun's come up over a thousand times." The Stage Manager tells you what's been happening—the mountains cracked a little bit more and some babies who hadn't been born three years ago have started to talk in complete sentences. Things are placed side by side like in the first act—the small and the large, the trivial detail of everyday life and the enormous force of nature.

The Stage Manager also tells the audience that the first act was called "Daily Life." This one will be "Love and Marriage." He implies that the last act will be about death.

NOTE: Birth, marriage, and death   These are the three major crises of human existence according to Wilder. He believes that most people are so caught up in the everyday small events, like the weather and stringing beans, that they fail to see the real grandeur and terror of life as it passes. It is only when one of these three crises occurs that people stand back and take a look at being alive. Usually, at these times, it's impossible to avoid being aware of the importance of the event. At other times, Wilder believes, we live out our lives in a state of self-imposed blindness.

The date is July 7, 1904, and it's been raining. Otherwise, this morning seems to begin very much the same way that the morning of Act I began—the 5:45 train has blown its whistle, and Mrs. Webb and Mrs. Gibbs are fixing breakfast.

The Stage Manager points out that "both of those ladies cooked three meals a day—one of 'em for twenty years, the other for forty—and no summer vacation. They brought up two children apiece, washed, cleaned the house,—and *never a nervous breakdown*. It's like what one of those Middle West poets said: You've got to love life to have life, and you've got to have life to love life. . . . It's what they call a vicious circle."

NOTE: The poet and woman's place The midwest poet is Edgar Lee Masters, and the poem is "Lucinda Matlock." Lucinda, the narrator of the poem, lived to ninety-six, working hard, taking care of her family (like Mrs. Gibbs and Mrs. Webb), and enjoying every minute of it. She ends by saying:

> What is this I hear of sorrow and weariness,
> Anger, discontent, and drooping hopes?
> Degenerate sons and daughters,
> Life is too strong for you—
> It takes life to love life.

Is Wilder saying that women are happiest working hard and taking care of their families? Or is he saying that *people* are happiest working hard and taking care of their families? What do you think?

The "action" begins with the milkman and the newspaper boy (Joe's younger brother Si, this time), and they talk about a wedding and the weather. Look back to the beginning of Act I. They talked about the same things then, and Joe wasn't any more enthusiastic about marriage than his brother is now. Why do you suppose Wilder uses this kind of repetition?

Howie delivers the milk to Mrs. Webb and Mrs. Gibbs, and at each house you hear the same conversation about the weather and the wedding. If you hadn't guessed long ago, you now know that Emily and George are getting married.

Over breakfast, Mrs. Gibbs worries about the wedding ("they're too *young*") and the doctor reminisces about being a groom and his fears that he and his wife would run out of things to talk about.

The talk is typical of the kinds of things people say before weddings. The doctor's words are sentimental and nostalgic, but Mrs. Gibbs's words are quite different. She says, "Weddings are perfectly awful things. Farces,—that's what they are!" Wilder's feeling that marriage is neither all good nor all bad but a mixture of both is typical of his understanding of human relationships. You will meet this double perception again in the play.

The parents have a bit of trouble trying to think of their son as an adult—"that great gangling thing!" says the doctor. And when George comes down and wants to run across to see Emily, his mother makes him put on his overshoes.

It's all very typical, parents having trouble realizing that their children are growing up. But before you start thinking of it as overly sentimental, look again. Did you notice how many references to death there are in this little scene? George pretends to cut his throat; Mrs. Gibbs keeps talking about his death of cold and says, "From tomorrow on you can kill yourself in all weathers." Why do you suppose Wilder did this? Is he preparing you for the next act? Is he saying that death is always a part of life? What do you think?

Mrs. Webb won't let George see Emily. Traditionally, a groom is not allowed to see his bride on the wedding day until the ceremony begins. That's just superstition, George protests, but Mr. Webb says, "There's a lot of common sense in some superstitions. . . ."

NOTE: Superstitions   Are customs and superstitions founded on common sense? Or do they just keep people from recognizing what life is like? A superstition will keep you on a known path that avoids risks. Do you have to step off the path to encounter the very best and worst of life? Is this what Wilder is saying?

You might want to consider the idea that customs keep people bound into a very narrow view of life. This idea is repeated near the end of the play by Emily. Can you identify any customs or superstitions in your life or in the lives of people you know? Do they put unnecessary limits on life?

The nervous groom sits down to a cup of coffee with Mr. Webb, the almost equally nervous future father-in-law. Mr. Webb makes various attempts at small talk and assures George that all men feel just the way he does. "A man looks pretty small at a wedding. . . . All those good women standing shoulder to shoulder making sure that the knot's tied in a mighty public way."

What do you think Wilder is saying? Is he suggesting that women want to marry and men don't? Or is he perhaps saying that relationships are difficult, and marriage keeps you from running away?

Is he poking gentle fun at men's and women's attitudes toward marriage?

NOTE: When *Our Town* was first produced, there was tremendous disagreement among the critics. Some saw this scene as satiric, others saw it as religious, and still others as an exercise in nostalgia. You should develop your own interpretation, supporting it with evidence from the play.

Mr. Webb next gives George the advice his own father had given him when he married—advice on how to keep your wife in line and show her who's in charge. George is a bit taken aback, but Mr. Webb goes on, "So I took the opposite of my father's advice and I've been happy ever since."

Is this another example of two views of an issue? Or is Wilder definitely on Mr. Webb's side? Perhaps Wilder is trying to nudge all men and women beyond immediate beliefs and attitudes to much larger issues? After all, he wanted to touch upon what is true for every person who exists. Doesn't *Our Town* have much less to do with particular people in a New England town than with the overall meaning of life?

To make sure things don't become too serious too soon, Wilder sends George home and has Mr. Webb offer his wife another superstition: "No bridegroom should see his father-in-law the day of the wedding or near it."

The Stage Manager interrupts again, dismissing the characters on stage. (He's a bit like the master of ceremonies in a variety show or the ringmaster

in a circus.) This time he wants to show you "how
this all began—this wedding, this plan to spend a
lifetime together." And he adds, "I'm awfully interested in how big things like that begin."

But before you see Emily and George, he wants
the people in the audience to reach back in their
memories to when they were young and in love.
Notice that two things are going on here. Wilder
is again encouraging the audience to feel a part of
what is happening, and he is suggesting that these
emotions are universal and that everyone experiences them.

NOTE: The manipulation of time   Wilder has been
playing with time all through the play. In the first
act, verb tenses shifted back and forth almost at
once. You were told what would happen to characters in their future (but in the past for the audience). Professor Willard talked about the land
millions of years ago, and at the beginning of this
act the Stage Manager described miniature changes
in mountains that will not have a noticeable effect
until far in the future. Each wrenching of time prepares you for the next. The first changes were only
verbal; then changes were described. In the scene
that follows between Emily and George, you move
back in time only a few years. However, you actually view the scene as it took place. You are asked
to accept that you can move about in time. The
earlier manipulations of time prepare you for this
one, just as this one prepares you for an even larger
wrench in the final act. Wilder has deliberately or-
ganized the material of the play to create the
strongest impact on the audience.

The Stage Manager takes two chairs from the Gibbs's kitchen and arranges them back-to-back at center stage. He puts a plank across the backs of the chairs and two stools in front of that. This will serve as Morgan's Drugstore on Main Street.

NOTE: Scenery   Wilder said that too much scenery on stage interfered with the action of the play. He also felt that the impact of a play was stronger if the playgoer had to participate by using his or her imagination. Wilder was well aware that a bare stage was all the Greeks had needed for their great tragedies, and that Shakespeare had also used few props, depending on dialogue to set the scene. When *Our Town* was first produced in the late 1930s, the bare stage was a startling novelty. Most plays of the time used realistic stage sets. However, the bare stage subsequently was used by a fair number of other playwrights.

Emily and George, high school students again, come on stage. They call good-bye to other friends, but when George asks to carry Emily's books home, she seems a bit distant. George wants to know what's wrong. She has difficulty saying it but finally tells him that she doesn't like the way he's changed. Baseball seems to have made him "conceited and stuck-up."

Now both of them are miserable. George says he's glad she told him, because "it's hard for a fella not to have faults creep into his character." Emily thinks their fathers are perfect and can't see why George can't be, too. George is inclined to think that "men aren't naturally good; but girls are." Emily thinks it's the other way around.

Wilder wants us to see George and Emily as both very young, with foolish ideas about the opposite sex. He is not ridiculing his characters (poking a little gentle fun at them, maybe), but reminding people in the audience that they were once young and foolish, too. The mood created here is one of nostalgia for a time remembered as wonderful but, when seen from the vantage point of adulthood, recognized as a little silly. Even if they are a bit silly, George and Emily are certainly idealistic. They seem to think people should try to be perfect.

Emily is so upset at the thought that she might have upset George that he takes her into the drugstore for an ice cream soda. So she won't be embarrassed, when the Stage Manager/Mr. Morgan asks if she's been crying, George says she was almost run over by a wagon.

Now George and Emily have one of those conversations that sound trivial to outsiders but are of tremendous importance to the people involved. George asks Emily to write to him while he's at State Agricultural College. She wonders if he'll lose interest in Grover's Corners once he goes away. He says that if that's a possibility, perhaps he shouldn't go. "I guess new people aren't any better than old ones," he says. So George decides to stay.

NOTE: Leaving home   You'll have to decide whether George is making a good choice here. By deciding to remain at home and become a farmer right away, is he giving up the chance to see life

in a broader perspective? Is he getting so caught
up in his immediate concerns that he won't have
a chance to see that life is bigger than this? Or is
he right? Would going away be the same as staying
at home because home and away are all the same?

George tries to explain to Emily that he wants
to stay because of the way he feels about her. In
half-spoken sentences, they manage to express what
they mean. "Would you be . . . I mean: *could* you
be. . . ," he says. "I . . . I am now; I always have
been," she answers.

You don't really need to see any more of their
courtship. Everyone can fill in the rest, from books,
movies, and personal experience. But there's another reason Wilder stops here. Some readers believe that the play is an allegory, that the characters and events in the play are personifications of
abstract ideas. An allegory tries to create a dual
interest both in the actual characters and events
being shown and in the abstract ideas being rep-
resented. This would explain why the characters
are not very individualized, why, for example, there
is little to distinguish Mrs. Webb from Mrs. Gibbs.

In the same way, Emily and George represent
every girl and boy who have ever fallen in love. If
you saw their relationship develop in distinctive
ways, George and Emily would become unique and
special and would no longer represent everyone.

The scene in the drugstore ends quickly. George
doesn't have enough money to pay and offers to
leave his gold watch until he can come back with
the money. Mr. Morgan says he will trust George
for ten years—"not a day over."

As in so many other scenes, when events threaten to become too emotional, Wilder ends this scene with a touch of humor. Does this keep you from viewing the events too seriously? Or does it keep you from viewing them too sentimentally?

Mr. Morgan turns back into the Stage Manager and announces that it's time for the wedding. The stage is rearranged to represent the church, and the Stage Manager has a chance to talk some more—to give a sermon this time, since he also plays the minister in the wedding scene. It's a brief sermon, but he brings in some important themes. He reminds you that marriage is part of the universal human experience and recognizes that people often feel confused when faced with a wedding, one of the major events of human life. "We thought that that ought to be in our play too," he says. This gives still another bit of emphasis to the idea that the people and events in this play represent human life in general.

Then he talks about the others involved in this wedding—the child who is yet to be born, and the ancestors, "millions of them." Past, present, and future are once more joined together.

He also talks about perfection—about the idea that "every child born into the world is nature's attempt to make a perfect human being." Not long ago you were listening to Emily and George talk about people trying to be perfect. They sounded a bit silly and naive. Now the idea has more serious overtones. Look for it to reappear in Act III.

It's time for the wedding to begin and time for the moment of panic. Mrs. Webb is upset—she never could bring herself to tell Emily "anything" before marriage. "I went into it blind as a bat myself," she adds. "The whole world's wrong, that's what's the matter."

Then three members of the baseball team appear. Their catcalls are filled with sexual innuendoes. The Stage Manager chases them away, smiling. "There used to be an awful lot of that kind of thing at weddings," he says. "We're more civilized now,—so they say."

Next comes George's moment of panic, his realization that life is passing. He doesn't want to grow old. But the moment passes and then it's Emily's turn. She also panics and wants to go back, wants to stay a little girl.

NOTE: Going back   There has been a lot of reminiscing on the part of the characters in this act. They have been looking back at the past and enjoying their memories. When Emily and George have their moments of panic here, they think of the past with fondness. You will see how different it will be in Act III when Emily does go back.

Seeing each other, both Emily and George recover and make their own promises before the ceremony—promising to care for each other, to love each other, to help each other. Why do you suppose these are the vows you hear, while Wilder has the traditional vows of the wedding service drowned out by Mrs. Soames' chatter?

NOTE: Creating an impact   Most plays begin by introducing characters, starting a sequence of events, and creating suspense about how the characters will fare. Suspense is not quite as important in *Our Town*. When you first see Emily and George, it seems clear they will marry. Suspense is created, however, by the fact that you know early in the play that someone will die in the last act, but you do not know who.

Instead of depending heavily on suspense, Wilder increases your emotional involvement. In Act I you watch the daily life of some people in a small town. It is pleasant. In Act II you participate in a courtship and a wedding. Your emotional involvement is heightened. Your involvement increases in the third, and final, act until the full impact of Wilder's ideas is revealed.

The actors all freeze in a tableau while the Stage Manager/Minister speaks of the pattern that marriage begins, a pattern that is repeated over and over again. Then the tableau is broken and the joyous bride and groom come down the aisle. Mrs. Soames has the final word—"The important thing is to be happy."

Do you think that Wilder agrees with Mrs. Soames? Or, since this is only one of the acts in the play, do you think he is saying that happiness is only one of the things that happens to people, not necessarily the most important? Are most of the people in the play happy or unhappy? Are they too busy to know? What do you think?

ACT III

During the intermission the audience sees the stagehands rearrange the set. Three rows of folding chairs are put on the right side of the stage, facing the audience. These represent graves in the cemetery.

NOTE: The popularity of *Our Town*   One of the reasons *Our Town* continues to be so popular with amateur groups is the ease with which it can be produced. There is very little expense involved. No elaborate sets or costumes are needed. And the simplicity of the empty stage, with the chairs being used to fill a variety of functions, is a striking visual metaphor about life.

But the ease of production is not the only reason for the play's popularity. *Our Town* shows us ourselves as we would like to believe we live. Life appears simple and pure. Almost everyone is good-natured and reasonably happy. Simon Stimson is the only character who has a terrible problem, and you never get to know him.

People like to believe that the picture *Our Town* represents is the way life is or can be. By setting the play in the relatively recent past, Wilder touched upon a common human feeling of nostalgia. The past frequently seems better than the present. Where were you even five years ago? Were you happier, younger, with fewer problems, with larger dreams for the future? The combination—life as we would like it to be, set in a simpler (and better) time than our own—has enormous appeal.

If Wilder had shown too much of Stimson's tale, you would be distracted from a story about George and Emily's innocence.

If Wilder had set the story further in the past, you might have difficulty relating to the lives of the characters. But everyone has walked home from

school with friends—or thinks that's the way life
should be. Wilder is showing us a picture of ourselves that we like to see. Audiences want to think
the play represents the essence of life.

As the intermission ends, some of the actors enter and sit in the chairs. Mrs. Gibbs and Simon
Stimson sit in the front row. A seat at the end
remains empty. In the second row is Mrs. Soames.
Wally Webb is in the third row.

NOTE: According to Wilder's stage directions,
the dead "do not turn their heads or their eyes to
right or left, but they sit in a quiet without stiff-
ness. When they speak their tone is matter-of-fact,
without sentimentality." Wilder wants the audience to notice that the dead have lost their emotional attachment to the living. Later, you will understand that even this becomes a comment on
what it means to be alive.

The Stage Manager takes up his usual position,
and when the house lights go down he begins to
speak. Nine years have gone by this time. And this
is a different part of Grover's Corners, "an important part," on a hilltop. He talks about the beauty
of the setting and points out the oldest graves,
belonging to the "strong-minded" settlers. Ge-
nealogists, paid by people who want to be certain
they have colonial ancestors, visit the graves.
"Wherever you come near the human race, there's
layers and layers of nonsense," he says. Then he

points out the Civil War veterans. "New Hampshire boys . . . had a notion that the Union ought to be kept together, though they'd never seen more than fifty miles of it themselves. . . . And they went and died about it."

Wilder is pointing out that humans are both silly and noble. There is no such thing as "either/or" when it comes to understanding the human race. It contains all possibilities.

Finally, the Stage Manager points to the actors sitting on chairs. Mrs. Gibbs, who worried so about her husband, is dead. So are Simon Stimson, Mrs. Soames, and Wally Webb.

NOTE: At the beginning of the play, the Stage Manager mentioned the deaths of several characters, including Mrs. Gibbs. It wasn't upsetting because you hadn't met them yet. And he didn't talk about every character's death. Now, learning about the death of Mrs. Gibbs and of Wally causes a pang. You've met them. They aren't just names any more. Why do you think Wilder has done this? You may recall the question, "How's it going to end?" Wilder wants you to realize that most people go through life asking such questions when they know the answer perfectly well. Everyone is going to die. Yet everyone acts as if death is unexpected.

Wilder uses the Stage Manager to state some other beliefs. "We all know that *something* is eternal. And it ain't houses and it ain't names. . . . That something has to do with human beings." There is, he says, something within each one of

us that lives on beyond our own life force. Is he
talking about the soul? The Stage Manager says
that all the great thinkers throughout history have
been saying it, but people have trouble remem-
bering the idea. "We all know," says the Stage
Manager. Is he right? Do we all know? Does Wilder
think we all know?

NOTE: Wilder has been accused of being too much
like a teacher, hitting you over the head with his
message. Do you think this is a valid criticism? Or
is the sugarcoating of humor and emotion thick
enough to make the message go down easily? Or
is Wilder raising questions rather than insisting on
certain answers?

In one of the most lyrical passages in the play,
the Stage Manager describes how the "earth part"
of people is burned away after death and the "eternal part" comes out. The part that attaches people
to the earth, memory and personal identity, has to
disappear. (This is why the actors in the chairs
speak and behave passively. The earth part of them
is burning out.) It is not that the dead cease to care
about the living; they hardly remember what it was
to be alive. Do you suppose that this is the perfection that people talked about earlier in the play?

Now the living appear. One is Joe Stoddard, the
undertaker, and the other is Sam Craig, a local boy
who moved out west—to Buffalo (a comic reminder of how small a small town can be).

Like the first two acts, this one begins in the
morning. But there is no train whistle, no milk-

man, no newspaper boy. And the exchange of news
this time is about the dead. As Sam looks at the
graves, Joe fills him in on what has happened.
Today's funeral is for Sam's cousin, a young person. You don't know right away who it is. When
Joe says that she died in childbirth, you suspect
that it was Emily, though you can't be completely
sure until Mrs. Gibbs tells you.

NOTE: **Death and childbirth** Dying in childbirth
was not uncommon before the need for sterile con-
ditions was realized. (In the same way, Wally's
burst appendix was invariably fatal before the dis-
covery of antibiotics.) But if all Wilder wanted was
to have Emily die, he had plenty of other options.
By having her die in childbirth, he emphasizes the
cycle of life that has been appearing all through
the play—birth, marriage, death, birth, marriage,
death, over and over again.

The funeral procession enters and moves to the
back of the stage on the left, most of them under
umbrellas.

NOTE: This scene has been described as one of
the most moving in modern drama. Try to envi-
sion the bare stage. On one side near the front are
the dead sitting in white chairs. They stare forward
passively. Diagonally across the stage, the mourners huddle under large, black umbrellas, almost
hidden from sight, trying to cope with the death
of someone they love.

The dead talk among themselves. Mrs. Soames, still chatty, remembers Emily, "one of the brightest girls ever graduated from High School." Remember Joe Crowell, the newsboy? Back in Act I the Stage Manager mentioned that he was "awful bright." He died in World War I, though. "All that education for nothing." Nobody, however, suggests that Emily's brightness went to waste. Is that because she married and had a child, repeating the cycle? Or is it because she was a woman? Does Wilder think that being bright isn't very important? What do you think?

As the group by the grave sings "Blest Be the Tie that Binds," Emily comes to take her place among the dead. The choir was singing that same hymn when Emily and George talked from their windows in the moonlight, and sang it again when Emily and George got married. Sung for the last time at Emily's funeral, the hymn has acquired a powerful emotional impact. But the impact is on the audience, not the dead, not even Emily. Already she feels as if her life had taken place thousands of years ago. To distract herself from the funeral, she begins to tell Mrs. Gibbs about the farm, and about the barn she and George built with the money Mrs. Gibbs left them.

___

NOTE: Things undone You may remember that in Act I, Mrs. Gibbs was going to sell a piece of furniture to raise the money for a trip to Paris. She never did take the trip, and eventually left the money to George and Emily—her "legacy" really did become a legacy. There are a variety of ways you could interpret this. Does Wilder want you to

regret that Mrs. Gibbs never did what she most
wanted? Is he saying that people don't take the
risks that would allow them to discover something
new, and that this is one of the things that makes
life so tragic? Or is he saying that the yearning for
something new makes people dissatisfied because
they fail to appreciate what they do have? Or is he
saying that there is no difference between places?

Emily continues to talk about her life. When she
looks at the mourners, she suddenly realizes that
they don't appreciate being alive. "They're sort of
shut up in little boxes," she says. Abruptly her
thoughts shift to her other child. "My little boy is
spending the day at your house," she tells one of
the dead. She doesn't quite realize yet that the
dead aren't interested. Emily still feels as if she is
one of the living, and it bothers her that they look
so troubled.

Suddenly, Emily realizes that she could return
to earth to relive her life. She senses it and although the dead try to discourage her, she per-
sists. The Stage Manager admits that she can return, but she is warned that it will be painful. She
will not only live her life again, but she will see
herself living it, and she will know the future.

NOTE: As we have seen, Wilder was influenced
by the Greeks. In an earlier novel, *The Woman of
Andros*, set in ancient Greece, a woman tells the
story of a dead young man who is allowed to re-
visit the earth. He must, however, pick the most
uneventful day in his life. Wilder was obviously

fascinated by the idea of the dead returning to life.
Many myths and legends deal with this theme.
Movies and television are also fond of the idea.
Have you ever seen any movies or television shows
that use this theme? Why do you think it has been
so appealing?

Emily still can't understand why returning to
earth will be so painful, but heeding the warnings
of the dead she picks a day that was not too important, her twelfth birthday.

The Stage Manager describes the day the same
way he opened the first act. "February 11th, 1899.
A Tuesday." Since Emily wants the whole day he
says, "We'll begin at dawn." This is a haunting
echo of the way the day began in the first two acts.
Suddenly, you are back on Main Street. This is the
strangest wrench in time yet. All through the play
you have been existing in two time periods at once—
the present and Grover's Corners time. Now you
are in three time periods at once—your own present,
Emily's past, and Emily's timeless existence in
death.

NOTE: In the directions for *Our Town*, Wilder
calls for the side of the stage to which Emily moves
when she visits her family to be very brightly lit.
He thought of it as "the brightness of a crisp win-
ter morning." Imagine the dead seated in pale light
while the other side of the stage is flooded with
bright light. The dead are present, but they do
nothing, they do not even react, while the "living"
go busily about their activities.

Using the same tone in which he introduced earlier scenes to the audience, the Stage Manager tells Emily that her mother will be coming down to make breakfast. You watch a scene you have seen twice before, but this time it is different. All your attention is focused on Emily. She has become the most important figure in the play, for she has taken the human journey that everyone takes. You have seen her life, and Wilder wants her now to embody your emotions and reactions. Emily watches Grover's Corners and you watch Emily. Both of you are coming to an understanding of what all those moments in Act I and Act II were really about.

Emily sees Howie Newsome, the milkman, come down the street, and then the constable. "But he's *dead; he died,*" she cries. Her mixture of tenses harkens back to the opening of the play.

What Wilder has been building toward is clear. Emily now carries with her an understanding of past, present, and future time. Wilder thinks that events that happened in the past or those that haven't happened yet—no matter how trivial—are important and deserve attention. The tiniest moments of everyday life are full of the essence of being alive.

NOTE: Some critics say *Our Town* is really a modern-day myth. Myth has its roots in the most basic beliefs of a people and presents a supernatural event as a way to interpret or understand a natural event concerning humanity or the cosmos. Characters and setting in myth are recognized as not necessarily real but as representing reality. For example, the myth of "King Midas and the Golden Touch" is not about a real king but about greed and its effects on people. Do you agree that Wilder is creating a myth in *Our Town*?

Emily tries to call to her mother and is struck painfully by how young her mother looks. Then Emily calls out that she can't find her hair ribbon. Now that she says exactly what she said fourteen years ago, her mother can hear her.

NOTE: Keep in mind what the Stage Manager told Emily about revisiting her life—she will not only see it, she will also be a part of it. The actress who plays Emily must say these lines like a twelve-year-old, but must also somehow manage to remain isolated while standing in the midst of the scene. Mrs. Webb is so busy making breakfast that she doesn't notice anything odd about her daughter's behavior. When this scene is played there is not even the table and chairs that served as props in the first two acts. The pantomime that Mrs. Webb and the others perform while Emily watches has a dreamlike quality to it.

Mr. Webb comes down the street and Emily whispers, "Papa." She is beginning to understand. Watching her parents, she can hardly bear the fact that they are so young and beautiful. Remember the conversation Emily had with her mother while stringing the beans? Then she didn't really want to hear about her mother's youth. Now both of you and she can appreciate the moment that was wasted. Wilder says that when you understand death, the small moments in life become precious.

It all becomes increasingly unbearable for Emily as she goes into breakfast and sees the presents from her family and George. She cries out to her mother that she is dead and reminds her of all that has happened. Now, at this moment, while we're happy, she says, *"Let's look at one another."* But of course Mrs. Webb can't hear her and doesn't look.

Emily can't stand it any longer. "It goes so fast," she says. "We don't have time to look at one another." She begins to cry. The bright light fades. Mrs. Webb disappears.

Now comes Emily's famous farewell to the world, ending with, "Oh, earth, you're too wonderful for anybody to realize you." Now Emily knows what the dead understand. She returns to her place among the dead. "Human beings," she says, are "blind people."

Simon Stimson picks up on the idea of blindness and embellishes it into the most bitter speech of the play. He remembers people in ignorance, trampling the feelings of others, "always at the mercy of one self-centered passion or another. . . . Ignorance and blindness."

Is this the way life seemed to you, looking at the people in Grover's Corners? Most of them seemed fairly loving and considerate. Why is Simon here, giving this speech? Mrs. Gibbs immediately responds, "that ain't the whole truth and you know it." But instead of explaining, she turns to the stars. Or is that an explanation in itself?

George appears and throws himself on Emily's grave. This time Emily is no longer upset because he is troubled and unhappy. She only says, "They don't understand, do they?"

"They don't understand, do they?"

Charles Steckler

The Stage Manager slowly draws a black curtain across the scene—the first time a curtain has been used in the play. But when he begins to talk it's about the Grover's Corners you're used to, with most people asleep and a train going by. Then there are the stars and earth's place in the Universe. There's no life on all those stars. Only this one is "straining away all the time," so that "every sixteen hours everybody lies down and gets a rest." And then he tells the audience, "You get a good rest, too."

The cycle is complete. The play began with morning, with people getting up, and ends at night, with people going to sleep. It began with birth and ends with death. It began with trivialities and ends with eternity.

A STEP BEYOND

Tests and Answers

TESTS

Test 1

1. Wilder's main theme in *Our Town* is that _____
   A. love conquers all
   B. the small things in life are important
   C. good triumphs over evil

2. One of the questions asked by people in _____
   the audience deals with
   A. social injustice   B. industrialization
   C. the power structure

3. Wilder believed that _____
   A. everyone should get married
   B. death was not the most important
      thing for humans to fear
   C. life throughout the ages is the same

4. A famous quotation from the play is _____
   A. "Love is blind"
   B. "I'll cry tomorrow"
   C. "People were made to live two by
      two"

5. Wilder borrowed some of his theatrical de- _____
   vices from
   A. Greek drama
   B. contemporary American drama
   C. classic French drama

6. In *Our Town* Wilder is mostly concerned _____
   with

A. birth, life, and death
B. relationships between young people
C. small-town life

7. Wilder wanted the audience to   ———
   A. participate in the play by using its
      own imagination
   B. relax, watch the play, and have a
      good time
   C. suffer the anguish of the situation
      along with the actors

8. The characters in the play value   ———
   A. love   B. wealth   C. power

9. In *Our Town* the characters   ———
   A. resist their fate
   B. strive to be heroic in their own lives
   C. are blind to the beauty of life

10. Wilder wants us to see Emily and George   ———
    as
    A. ill-fated lovers
    B. representative of everyone's youth
    C. in-depth studies of characters

11. Demonstrate the influence of the Greek drama on
    Wilder.

12. Discuss *Our Town* as an allegory.

13. Discuss Wilder's use of dual vision in *Our Town*.

14. Give three examples of Wilder's manipulation of time
    in the play. Explain why you think he manipulates
    time.

15. Why does Wilder use an almost empty stage for *Our
    Town*?

Test 2

1. Wilder believed that "real life" was _____
   A. always similar   B. basically political
   C. a struggle for survival

2. Wilder's characters are _____
   A. flesh-and-blood people
   B. allegorical
   C. thinly disguised political symbols

3. The dead tell Emily to _____
   A. return to the living
   B. express her grief
   C. not return to the living

4. Emily is able to _____
   A. rise from the dead
   B. visit her family for one day after she's
      dead .
   C. communicate with George after death

5. Wilder says the dead _____
   A. are afraid of the living
   B. have the earth part burned out
   C. hide from the living

6. The dead in *Our Town* _____
   A. have an influence on the living
   B. can affect the future
   C. understand what the living seldom
      can

7. Grover's Corners is _____
   A. a town Wilder once visited
   B. an archaeological site
   C. an imaginary place

8. Wilder used a bare stage because he   _____
   A. wanted to be an individualist
   B. did not want to limit the implications
      of the play
   C. was trying to make a statement about
      poverty

9. Wilder was convinced that   _____
   A. life is boring
   B. most people believe in the eternal
   C. people should be married in church

10. An important theme in *Our Town* is   _____
    A. the survival of the fittest
    B. nature's love of humanity
    C. man's relationship to the eternal

11. Discuss three of the most important themes in the
    play.

12. Why has *Our Town* remained so popular a play?

13. Define myth and explain why *Our Town* may be
    considered a myth.

14. Discuss Wilder's dependence on emotion rather than
    suspense to move the play forward.

15. In what ways did Wilder influence later dramatists?

ANSWERS

Test 1

1. B   2. A   3. C   4. C   5. A   6. A
7. A   8. A   9. C   10. B

11. Wilder was very interested in ancient Greek philosophy and drama, and you can see the Greek influence
in *Our Town*. Wilder made use of the Stage Manager in
much the same way that the ancient Greeks used the

chorus on stage. The Greek chorus often gave background information, offered advice to the actors and the
audience, foretold the future of characters, and knew all
about the past. During the opening scene, the Stage
Manager offers information to the audience about the
characters and discusses the time and place in which the
play is set. Much like the Greek chorus, he also comments on the action of the play. He suggests the importance of seeing life as beautiful, and near the play's
climax offers advice to Emily. Greek drama was concerned with enlightening its audience about universal
concerns, and Wilder has similar goals. Any deaths or
tragedies that took place in Greek drama happened off
stage. It was reported to have happened but never seen.
We are informed of Emily's death and all of the others
in the same way. The Stage Manager also plays several
small parts in the play, just as members of the Greek
chorus did.

12. A piece of literature is called an allegory when the
characters, setting, and events represent abstract ideas.
Allegory tries to create an interest in the characters, setting, and events being shown as well as in the abstract
ideas it is attempting to convey. The characters in *Our
Town* are not flesh-and-blood people but rather representative of experiences which all people have. For example, there is little to distinguish Mrs. Webb from Mrs.
Gibbs. One woman could easily be substituted for the
other without much change in the story. Each woman
is intended to convey the idea of mother and wife and
to stand for the experience of all women's lives. All of
the characters in the play, and the story itself, can be
understood in the same way.

13. Wilder's dual vision is seen throughout the play. He
juxtaposes the vastness of the universe and the small-

ness of people. In Act I, Professor Willard discusses different archaeological ages. The birth of the twins is mentioned right after this. In Act II, before the Stage Manager marries Emily and George, he reminds the audience that millions and millions of people have been married. Wilder makes these contrasts not to show people as insignificant but rather to point out that the daily activities of all people in all times link humanity together. Wilder also has his characters comment about human events such as weddings. Some think weddings are awful, while others believe they are wonderful. Wilder understands that human life is a profound and complicated mixture of both wonderful and awful. For example, when war is discussed it is seen as both a noble cause and a foolish affair.

14. There are many instances of the manipulation of time in *Our Town*. In Act I, the Stage Manager tells the audience about the future deaths of characters in the play. In Act II, just before the wedding, Wilder uses a flashback to show how Emily and George fell in love. After Emily's death, she returns in time to her twelfth birthday. Wilder's purpose in manipulating time is to keep the audience from trying to watch *Our Town* as a realistic play about a certain girl and boy who grow up and fall in love. Instead, Wilder wanted the audience to realize that this love story was happening over and over throughout history. *Our Town* is Wilder's attempt to tell a universal tale that stands outside a particular time and place. By moving back and forth in time, the audience is able to drop the inclination to view the play in just one way.

15. Wilder was not interested in showing a particular town and the lives of certain people. He wanted to tell a universal story about life itself that encompassed all

time and all places. He saw that each person, no matter when he or she lived, experienced birth, love, and death. Wilder attempted to convey that idea by using a bare stage. He felt that a set cluttered with realistic objects that attempted to create a real place, such as a Victorian home, would bind the story to that time and place. He used a bare stage to create a sense of the universal, allowing the audience to fill in whatever it wanted to imagine. For the same reason, the play requires hardly any props and the actors usually wear regular street clothing. Without anything extra on stage, the play transcends time and place.

Test 2

1. A   2. B   3. C   4. B   5. B   6. C
7. C   8. B   9. B   10. C

11. Love is the strongest theme in the play. Wilder shows the power of, and need for, love among humans. He also demonstrates how people live almost oblivious to the importance of love relationships. It is only in death that people realize how much or how little they have loved someone and how irreversible that loss is. Every human relationship has some element of love to it. After Emily's death, she revisits earth on her twelfth birthday, only to realize the importance of the love she felt, not only for her mother but for everyone. Another very obvious theme is the continuity of human life. Everyone is born, grows older, falls in love, and dies. Birth, life, and death are seen as natural stages of a cycle that every person travels through. Each act in *Our Town* mentions birth and death and deals with an important aspect of being alive. This cycle relates all people throughout time to one another. Wilder believed that we do not appreciate the beauty of daily existence. In Act I, Editor Webb

is asked what love of beauty and culture there is in
Grover's Corners. He replies that there's not much, but
that people do appreciate the sun coming over the
mountains every morning and enjoy watching the birds.
These seemingly small pleasures are, according to Wilder,
the beauty of life that is most often not appreciated.

12. *Our Town* has remained an extremely popular play
for several reasons. Simplicity of production is one. Because there is no need for an elaborate setting, no props
or costumes, the play is inexpensive to produce. It is
also a simple play to stage. Few stagehands are required,
and if necessary the actors can rearrange the chairs and
remove the furniture themselves. Wilder shows us ourselves as we would like to believe we can live our lives.
Life in *Our Town* is simple and wholesome. Everyone,
with the exception of Simon Stimson, is happy and good-
natured. Wilder has also created a wonderful feeling of
nostalgia by showing us a past we would like to believe
was better. The combination of seeing life as we would
like to think it is and feeling nostalgia for a lost time is
perfect. Wilder shows us what we hope is ourselves,
and most audiences like what they see.

13. A myth is a story that uses a supernatural event to
explain a basic or natural truth that is commonly ac-
cepted. *Our Town* concerns the appreciation of life and
being loved by other people. Wilder has Emily die and
return to observe the middle of her young life, unseen
by her family. It's only in this way that she comes to
appreciate the importance of love and life. The play takes
on mythical proportions during the final act when Emily
takes a journey after her death. Because of Wilder's skill
as a playwright, we are willing to believe in this supernatural event and be moved by it.

14. Most plays begin by introducing characters and a

conflict. The suspense normally moves the play along. Wilder relies on a somewhat different method. In *Our Town*, there is relatively little conflict or suspense. Instead, Wilder deals with little moments that display the essence of what it is to be alive. In the first act we see George and Emily talking from their windows while the choir sings "Blessed Be the Tie that Binds" in the background. In Act II we watch special moments that usually happen before a wedding. We see a mother worrying about her son for the last time, a father trying not to give advice, a nervous groom and bride. The same hymn is used again. These little moments combined with the music draw us to the characters and encourage us to remember our own experiences. When we hear the same hymn for the third time at Emily's funeral, we cannot help but be moved. Each of these essential moments builds on the others toward an emotional climax.

15. Although Wilder's plays are very different from those of the Theater of the Absurd movement, he did influence writers like Edward Albee who were producing plays in the early 1960s. Wilder, though not a rebel like the absurdist playwrights, did experiment with new techniques on the stage. He was interested in breaking the restrictions and limitations of the realistic stage setting. He wanted his plays to concern more than just one time and place. He used the bare stage, minimal props, and no costumes to create this effect of timelessness. Wilder was also concerned more with concepts and language than with action. All of these ideas were incorporated into the absurdist movement. Albee acknowledges Wilder as a master of experiment in the theater and has imitated some of his methods.

Term Paper Ideas and other Topics for Writing

Characters

1. Compare the function of the Stage Manager in *Our Town* to the Chorus in *Oedipus Rex*.

2. Examine the women characters in the play. What is the role of women in society as portrayed in *Our Town*?

3. How do characters in *Our Town* live blinded to the wonder of life? Give several examples.

4. How does Emily come to appreciate having been alive?

Literary Topics

1. How does Wilder manipulate time in the play?

2. Discuss the use of the universal and the particular view in *Our Town*. How does this relate to Wilder's ideas about mankind?

3. How does Wilder make use of nostalgia in the play?

4. In what ways can *Our Town* be considered a tragedy?

5. How can *Our Town* be seen as an allegory.

6. Is *Our Town* a didactic play? Does Wilder act more like a teacher than a playwright?

7. What is the significance of death in *Our Town*?

8. What is Wilder's concept of time? How is it important to the play?

9. Does *Our Town* take on the proportions of a myth?

10. What do you think is the artist's responsibility to society? Does Wilder live up to your definition?

Stagecraft

1. How does Wilder encourage the audience's participation in *Our Town*?

2. What effect does the lack of scenery have on the play?

3. How does Wilder create mood in *Our Town*? Why is it important?

4. How does Wilder achieve emotional impact in the play? In what ways are his techniques different from those of other playwrights?

5. How does Wilder use music and sound to heighten the effect of the play?

Sources and Influences

1. In what ways did Greek drama influence Wilder's thinking and writing?

2. How did Wilder and his techniques influence the playwrights of the Theater of the Absurd?

3. Which events in Wilder's life may have led him to the theories set forth in *Our Town*?

4. Examine a playwright (for instance, Edward Albee) who was influenced by Wilder's work.

Further Reading
CRITICAL WORKS

Brown, John Mason. "Wilder: *Our Town*." *Saturday Review of Literature*, August 6, 1949, p. 34.

Burbank, Rex J. *Thornton Wilder*. Boston: G. K. Hall, 1978.

Corrigan, Robert W. "Thornton Wilder and the Tragic Sense of Life." *Educational Theater*, October 1961, pp. 167–173.

Fergusson, Francis. "Three Allegorists: Brecht, Wilder and Eliot." *Sewanee Review*, Fall 1956, pp. 544–73.

Fuller, Edmund. "Thornton Wilder: The Notation of a Heart." *American Scholar*, September 1959, pp 210–217.

Goldstein, Malcolm. *The Art of Thornton Wilder*. Lincoln, Nebraska: University of Nebraska Press, 1965.

Goldstone, Richard H. *Thornton Wilder: An Intimate Portrait*. New York: E. P. Dutton, 1975.

Grebanier, Bernard. *Thornton Wilder*. Minneapolis: University of Minnesota Press, 1964.

Haberman, Donald. *The Plays of Thornton Wilder: A Critical Study*. Middletown, Connecticut: Wesleyan University Press, 1967.

Harrison, Gilbert S. *The Enthusiast*. New York: Ticknor & Fields, 1983.

Kuner, M. C. *Thornton Wilder: The Bright and the Dark*. New York: Thomas Y. Crowell, 1972.

Stresau, Hermann. *Thornton Wilder*. New York: Frederick Ungar, 1971.

AUTHOR'S OTHER WORKS

The Cabala, 1926 novel
The Bridge of San Luis Rey, 1927 novel
The Angel That Troubled the Waters and Other Plays, 1928
The Woman of Andros, 1930 novel
The Long Christmas Dinner and Other Plays in One Act, 1931
Heaven's My Destination, 1935 novel
The Merchant of Yonkers, 1939 play
The Skin of Our Teeth, 1942 play
Our Century, 1947 play

The Ides of March, 1948 novel
The Alcestiad, with a Satyr Play, The Drunken Sisters, 1957
The Eighth Day, 1967 novel
Theophilus North, 1973 novel
American Characteristics and Other Essays, 1979

The Critics

On Allegory

He [Wilder] hardly imagines them [the characters]
as people, he rather invites the audience to accept
them by plainly labelling them; they are sentimental
stereotypes of village folksiness. They are therefore
understandable by the greater number, and they
serve to present the story and illustrate the moral.

This type of allegory is perfectly in accord with
the Platonic kind of philosophy which it is designed
to teach. The great Ideas are timeless, above the
history of the race and the history of actual individuals. Any bit of individual or racial history will do,
therefore, to "illustrate" them; but history and individual lives lack all real being: they are only shad-
ows on the cave wall.

—*Francis Fergusson*, Three
    Allegorists: Brecht, Wilder and
    Eliot, 1956

On Life and Love

Wilder has always been on the side of life and life
is seen to be most directly affirmed through love.
Love, then, is his most persistent theme and it has
been for him an inexhaustible subject.

—*Robert W. Corrigan, "Thornton
    Wilder And The Tragic Sense of
    Life,"* 1961

Wilder on Wilder

Our Town is not offered as a picture of life in a New
Hampshire village; or as a speculation about con-

ditions of life after death (that element I merely took
from Dante's *Purgatory*). It is an attempt to find a
value above all price for the smallest events of our
daily life. I have made the claim as preposterous as
possible, for I have set the village against the largest
dimensions of time and place. The recurrent words
in the play (few have noticed it) are "hundreds,"
"thousands," and "millions." Emily's joys and griefs,
her algebra lessons and her birthday present—what
are they when we consider all the billions of girls
who have lived, who are living and who will live?
Each individual's assertion to an absolute reality can
only be inner, very inner. And here the method of
staging finds its justification—in the first two acts
there are at least a few chairs and tables; but when
Emily revisits the earth and the kitchen to which
she descended on her twelfth birthday, the very
chairs and tables are gone. Our claim, our hope,
our despair are in the mind—not in things, not in
"scenery.". . . The climax of this play needs only
five square feet of boarding and the passion to know
what life means to us.
                    —*Thornton Wilder*, American
                      Characteristics And Other
                      Essays, 1979

The Tragic Vision
The vision Wilder offers of the human condition in
Our Town is essentially tragic. It is a picture of the
priceless value of even the most common and rou-
tine events in life and of the tragic waste of life
through failure to realize the value of every moment. Unaware of the value of life, the people of
Grover's Corners live their lives banally and seldom
get beneath or above the surface of life.
    The artistic problem basic to *Our Town* is that of
showing that the events of life are at once not all
they could be because they are taken for granted—
but are priceless. . . . By relating the ordinary events
in the lives of these ordinary people to a meta-
physical framework that broadens with each act, he
is able to portray life as being at once significant

and trivial, noble and absurd, miraculous and humdrum.

—*Rex J. Burbank*, Thornton Wilder,
1978

On *Our Town*

If he [Wilder] did away with scenery and relied on
a stage manager to set his stage, it was because the
human heart was his real scene. It was the heart of
the community which he laid bare.

In the thirties, tingling as they were with social
consciousness, there were those who complained. . . . They could not believe in *Our Town*
because it lacked brothels, race riots, front-page
scandals, social workers, agitators, and strikes. The
passing years, however, have only proved Mr.
Wilder's correctness in writing as he did. His subject had no datelines. His interest was not what gets
into the public prints. It was what each of us must
live with in private. Man's spirit was his business;
man's spirit and evocations of those small-impor-
tant incidents which test us in our daily living.

—*John Mason Brown*, "Wilder: Our
Town," 1949

Wilder's Use of Time and Memory

By recalling past time, Wilder has, in the three acts
of his play, created his own time separate from that
time of the audience which ticks away each minute.
He has presented in recognizable sequence birth,
marriage, and death, events analogous to the cycle
of life of any member of the audience. . . . The repeated shifts in time are reminders that all parts of
life's sequence are in operation for any number of
people at any time. It is the force of memory that is
always in the present tense. This memory, juggling
all the events at once like a circus performer, keeps
the action in the eternal *now* on stage.

—*Donald Haberman*, The Plays of
Thornton Wilder, 1967

On Language

The problem Wilder set for himself was to find a language recognizable as ordinary middle-class speech but still able to convey feeling and meaning. The dialogue is the speech of anyone, and that is the point. Clichés are clichés precisely because they are so very true on an elementary level. The absence of scenery and properties and the exploitation of the stage as stage both permit the clichéd dialogue and prevent it from being merely banal. The commonplace in such speech is returned to its pristine truth, as though it were being uttered for the first time, and the simple truth of family living is given new life.

—*Donald Haberman*, The Plays of
Thornton Wilder, 1967

On the Importance of Life

The meaning of life is revealed in living—hot bath water as well as great festivals—and that living must be done with an awareness that it can cease at any time. Life must not be lived as though it were a mere passage to something better. It cannot be embraced with reservation. The sorrow is that there is no permanence.

—*Donald Haberman*, The Plays of
Thornton Wilder, 1967